PRAISE FOR *DOSSIER: THE SECRET HISTORY OF ARMAND HAMMER*

Winner of the Financial Times / Booz Allen & Hamilton Global Business Book Award for both best biography and best business book for Dossier: The Secret History of Armand Hammer.

"In "Dossier: The Secret History of Armand Hammer," Edward Jay Epstein's fascinating, painstakingly researched book, Hammer's old life is revealed in fascinating detail, exposing him as the liar and conniver that he was/Among Epstein's more shocking revelations is that Hammer acted as a virtual spy for the Soviet Union, a conduit for money that financed Communist espionage operations."
-- *Los Angeles Times*

"Edward Jay Epstein opens his life of Armand Hammer with a line from Balzac: "Behind every great fortune there is a crime." He then goes on for some 400 absorbing pages to prove what a wise chap Balzac was, certainly in Hammer's case. Much of it reads, indeed, like a long-suppressed secret file. We already knew of the public Hammer, self-professed humanitarian, philanthropist, art patron. Now we have the Hammer of the dossier, a morbidly fascinating compound of ambition, greed, unscrupulousness and power hunger."
– *New York Times Book Review*

"Edward Jay Epstein's Dossier: The Secret History of Armand Hammer especially claims our gratitude because its protagonist would otherwise have been forgotten and his fortune, his monuments, and the whole huge mound of his frauds long since gone up in smoke."
--New York Review of Books

"Epstein found proof in Soviet archives that Armand Hammer, along with his Communist father Julius, used their business at the direction of Soviet intelligence to funnel money to operatives abroad. The Russian art Hammer peddled in the West in the 1930s was not, as he claimed, his own. It had been looted from estates and churches by the Bolshevik regime, which sold it through Hammer to generate hard currency."
--Baltimore Sun

ALSO BY EDWARD JAY EPSTEIN

Inquest: The Warren Commission and the Establishment of Truth

Counterplot: Garrison vs. the United States

News from Nowhere: Television and the News

Between Fact and Fiction: The Problem of Journalism

Agency of Fear: Opiates and Political Power in America

Cartel: A Novel

Legend: The Secret World of Lee Harvey Oswald

The Rise and Fall of Diamonds: The Shattering of a Brilliant Illusion

Who Owns the Corporation?: Management vs. Shareholders

Deception: The Invisible War Between the KGB and the CIA

The Annals of Unsolved Crime

Dossier: The Secret History of Armand Hammer

The Big Picture: Money and Power in Hollywood

How America Lost Its Secrets: Snowden, the Man and the Theft

T H E HAMMER DOSSIER

THE DARK SIDE OF POWER

BY EDWARD JAY EPSTEIN

© Copyright ©) by E.J.E Publication

Ltd, Inc 2011,2021

All rights reserved.

Parts of this book appeared in earlier form in *The New Yorker*

For Susana Duncan

CONTENTS

Preface   Meeting Armand Hammer

PART ONE   THE HAMMER INVESTIGATION

PART TWO   THE DEATH MARCH

PART THREE   THE ART OF THE BRIBE

PART FOUR   THE HAMMER GENERATIONS

EPILOGUE

Preface

Meeting Dr. Hammer

I first met Armand Hammer on February 21, 1981 at his office on the top floor of the Occidental headquarters in Los Angeles. The octogenarian founder and chairman of the company spryly raced around his desk, extended his arm and with an iron-grip handshake introduced himself as "Dr. Hammer."

I was there to write a profile of him for the *New York Times Magazine*. He was just beginning his campaign to win the Nobel Peace Prize and, since he was on friendly terms with Arthur "Punch" Sulzberger, the chairman and publisher of the *Times*, he assumed that I would present him favorably. He immediately asked if I knew Punch and when I said I did not, he offered to take me to dinner with him (and he eventually did). He also told me that he assumed that the story would be featured on the cover of the *Times* magazine, and he suggested that if I had "any problems" with my editor at the magazine, he would "call Punch" on my behalf. He clearly liked to believe he was in control and at the time, I did nothing to disillusion him.

  On a personal level, I found Hammer to be a modest and affable man, who far more closely resembled a country doctor than a corporate magnate. To get to know him, He suggested that I travel with him on his private jetliner, Oxy One, on his non-stop business and political trips. And I did. The Oxy One, a Boeing 737 airliner which had been specially designed for intercontinental flight, was a very comfortable way to travel. It had a 100-foot-long cabin configured as a personal salon. His bedroom, which he shared with his wife Frances, had twin beds and a shower. Next to it was an office, and behind that was the guest quarters, where I stayed. We would drive right onto the tarmac in a convoy of limousines and, as the crew snapped to attention, we would board the plane.

In the course of the next six months, I traveled with Hammer to Paris, London, Ottawa, Chicago, L.A, Washington D.C. and New York, where he enjoyed prestigious hotels, in particular Claridge's in London, the Plaza Athenee in Paris and the Madison in Washington D.C. Despite his wealth, he seemed to relish being recognized by the hotel employees. He also enjoyed going to the more celebrated restaurants, such as the Tour d'Argent in Paris and Wilton's in London, but once there he had little tolerance for gourmet food, often preferring to order a hamburger.

During these trips, I spent scores of hours discussing his life, achievements and business strategies. It was not always easy. He was slightly hard of hearing, and he used this infirmity to great effect when he did not want to discuss an issue. When I asked

Hammer questions he did not expect or want to answer, he simply ignored them. He also wore thick glasses that did not entirely correct his severe myopia. As a result, like the Mr. Magoo character in the cartoon series, often he did not recognize acquaintances. When he crossed time zones in Oxy One, he had little respect for other people's sleep. He had no inhibitions about calling subordinates at home in the middle of the night. He kept his own schedule, napping or working, to suit his convenience. His third wife Francis almost always accompanied him on these trips and acted as his help mate. When the plane landed, he was usually met by a raft of personal assistants, public relations men, security men and his personal photographer, whom he instructed when to take pictures. This sizable entourage, which I often had strain to keep up with him, gave him more the appearance of a visiting head of state than a mere corporate executive.

    Throughout the winter and spring of 1981, Hammer took me with him to a constant stream of events of which he made himself the center of attention. In New

York, he invited me, as well as my girlfriend Laurie Frank, to an extraordinary dinner party he was hosting at Lincoln Center for Prince Charles, the crown prince of Great Britain. He sat me between Punch Sulzberger and Nancy Reagan, who was then First Lady, while he sat next to the Prince of Wales. He seemed in complete control of the royal prince, tugging him around the table to make introductions. He also invited me to diplomatic receptions, award-ceremonies, museum openings, private parties, press conferences and charity events. Aside from Punch Sulzberger, Prince Charles and Nancy Reagan, he introduced me to such acquaintances as Bob Hope, Al Gore, Louis Nizer, Senator Charles Percy, Edgar Faure, Sir John Foster, Prince Bandour Bin Sultan of Saudi Arabia, David Murdock, and Pierre Trudeau. His purpose was to provide me with colorful material for a story in which, as he conceived of it, he would be a central actor in a rarefied universe of money, altruism and power.

After he had bought Leonardo Da Vinci's codex at auction in London and promptly renamed it the *Hammer Codex*. He suggested I accompany him back to London for the handover.

In London, he stayed at Claridge's and suggested I join him in the dining room but, since he was not wearing a tie, the headwaiter refused to seat him. Infuriated, Hammer booked a suite just for us to eat in and ordered the dinner from room service. The next morning he used a news conference to commemorate his purchase of the Da Vinci Codex. To call attention to its value, he arranged for four Chinese guards supposedly trained in kung fu to surround it. The codex was then put into an armored car, which followed Hammer's Rolls to Oxy One at the airport.

With the Codex in tow, we flew to Paris, where Hammer had a meeting at the Plaza Athenee. He left the Codex aboard the plane, telling me, with a chuckle, that the kung fu guards were "just for show." Hammer did not himself carry credit cards. That was the job of his assistant, James Pugash. The next morning, when we checked out, the Plaza Athenee refused to accept Pugash's credit card, and Hammer flew into a rage when the hotel held up the delivery of baggage to his waiting limousine until he paid.

When by summer, I still had not completed the story for *the New York Times*, he grew so impatient that offered to help me write the story. I thanked him for his interest but I did not tell him what was delaying its completion was my efforts to gather information about the darker side of his life.

I was then in the midst of writing my book *Deception: The Invisible War Between the KGB and CIA*, about espionage . One of my sources for this book was James Jesus Angleton, the former CIA counterintelligence chief, who, suggested to me that I might find "another side" of Hammer's activities by examining Soviet trade mission documents seized by British intelligence agents in 1927. Through my very able British-born researcher, Rebecca Fraser, I managed to obtain these documents. They, in turn, led to files in the National Archives concerning investigation of the Hammer family business in the 1920s which, though they contained more questions than answers, indicated that Hammer had begun his career laundering money and art for the Soviet Union. After I told him about what my researcher had found, he had his lawyer Arthur Groman take action to seal, if not expunge, these files at the National Archives.

I was also blocked necause I did not have access to Hammer's FBI file. I sued under the The Freedom of Information Act but it only allowed access if the subject is deceased. Nevertheless, I had found enough in Hammer's past show that Hammer was not all that he claimed to be

The story published in the *New York Times Magazine* in November 1981 posed the question: Does Hammer merely take advantage of his contacts with the Russians to advance his business interests or does Hammer take advantage of his business contacts to serve Moscow's interest? It so infuriated Hammer that he wrote a twenty-five page letter to Punch and the editor of the Times describing himself in the way that he wanted to be described in the article. He demanding the editors publish it in full, but instead they ran only a short excerpt in the letters-to-the-editor section.

Even though my personal relation with Hammer ended with the publication of the *Times* article, my curiosity about him was not yet quenched.

PART ONE
THE HAMMER INVESTIGATION

My interest with Armand Hammer
began in September 1980 in a guest house
on a remote island in the Java Sea in which

the apex predators were 8-foot long Komodo dragons. The guesthouse belonged to Natomas, a San Francisco-based petroleum company with offshore oil concessions in the Java sea. I had been invited there by Dorman Commons, the chairman of Natomas, to see Natomas' oil operations in Indonesia. After dinner, over Cuban Montecristo cigars, the conversation turned to Armand Hammer for two reasons. First, he was in the news. It was reported by Reuters that Hammer, now 82, was a candidate for the Nobel Peace Prize because of the good relations he had fostered between America and the Soviet Union. And second, before joining Natomas, Commons had worked for Hammer as the chief financial officer of Occidental Petroleum, the oil company that Hammer had built from a tiny Californian one-rig driller into an international behemoth in the 1960s and 1970s. When Commons scoffed at the idea of him succeeding at bringing about peace, I asked him how he had succeeded so spectacularly in the oil business. Commons, leaning forward in his bamboo chair, whispered, "Bribes."

I asked him how one goes about building an international oil giant like Occidental through bribery.

He answered, "With Hammer, it is high art. From what I saw in Libya, he is the true Nijinsky of bribery." He then proceeded to lay out the entire scheme by which Hammer corrupted the entire entourage of King Idris of Libya to get the major oil concession in the Libyan Desert that made Hammer's fortune.

The next issue was how Hammer kept these concessions after Muammar Gaddafi overthrew King Idris in 1969?

Commons answered that he understood that the Russians, who supported Gaddafi's revolution, helped Hammer after Gaddafi took over.

"Did Hammer also bribe the Russians?" I asked.

Commons shrugged, showing the palms of both his hands and said he was not privy to Hammer's relationship with the Russians. "Who was? I asked?

He said that he understood that Hammer had employed John Burton Tigrett for such sensitive missions.

Born in 1913 in Jackson, Tennessee, Tigrett was a highly-resourceful entrepreneur who met Hammer in the mid-1960s. I later met him through a mutual friend, Sir James Goldsmith, who invited us both to his home in Cuxemala, Mexico in 1986. Tigrett, who had been Hammer's bagman for nearly two decades, described to me how he had delivered attaché cases full of hundred dollars bills from a Swiss numbered account to Hammer's designated recipients. He said that in 1969 one of his first mission was delivering $100,000 in cash to Yekaterina Furtseva, the Soviet culture minister, who,in return. arranged for Hammer to obtain a Kasimir Malevich painting which Hammer promptly sold for $750,000. Tigrett said that the purpose of Hammer's bribe was not merely to obtain a painting but to gain a hold over Furtseva, who was a member of the Soviet politburo. Tigrett drew a global roadmap of the politicians Hammer had compromised . It extended from the Soviet Union to a dozen nations in Africa, Latin America, the United States and Europe. It included the cash in envelopes that Tigrett gave to a dozen Norwegian parliamentarians in return for their promise to vote for Hammer for the Nobel Peace Prize (which is awarded in Oslo by Norway's Parliament, the Storing.) Some of the illegal political payments he made on Hammer's behalf in the United States wound up implicating Hammer in the Watergate pay-off scandal. Even though the FBI investigated Hammer no fewer than six times for bribery, it failed to build a case that would stand up in court. Hammer was, as Tigrett told me, too good at covering his tracks.

   There remained one key piece in the jigsaw that remained missing. Hammer had spent nearly a decade in the 1920s dealing with Lenin's Communist regime in the Soviet Union at a time that the U.S was trying to destroy it. Although it was well known that he had met with Lenin and other top Soviet officials in Moscow, what services, if any, that Hammer performed for them, remained obscured by Soviet secrecy.

However, with the collapse of the Soviet Union in 1989, the KGB archives on Hammer's activities in Russia became available.

To find his file om these archives, I went to Moscow in 1991 on a trip organized by Victor Navasky, the owner of the *Nation*. The other invitees included Katrina vanden Heuvel, the *Nation's* managing director, Hamilton Fish, the head of the Nation and Carl Bernstein, co-author of *All The President's Men*. Because of the morass of red tape at the KGB archive, I contracted with East View Publications, a company that specializes in obtaining documents from Russian archives, to get the documents about Armand Hammer for me. It wound up costing about $30,000 but it was well worth the price. The East View research team in Moscow found 3,000 pages of classified Soviet documents in the KGB archive that described in considerable detail Hammer's relations with the Soviet authorities in the 1920s and early1930s. The documents revealed that his father Dr. Julius Hammer, one of the founders of the faction that evolved into the U.S. Communist Party, had been secretly working for Lenin in getting goods through the U.S. embargo, and he was supposed to come to Moscow in 1920. He could not make the trip because he had been sentenced to three and a half years in Sing Sing prison for performing an illegal abortion in New York. So his eldest son Armand, then a 22-year old medical student at Columbia, became his replacement.

Armand spent most of the next ten years in Moscow tending the family business which included laundering money and equipment through front companies to the still-embargoed Soviet Union. When he returned to the U.S. in the U.S, the Soviet Union used him to launder a vast trove of expropriated art objects. From this Hammer file, it became clear that he was a secret commercial asset of the Soviet government for at least two decades. This explained the origin of his apparent fortune and brings to mind Balzac's insight that behind every great fortune, there is a great crime.

PART TWO

THE HAMMER TAPES

Even though the FBI was unable to find evidence of Hammer's bribery, Hammer produced his own evidence by secretly recording many of his compromising conversations dealing with bribery and other murky activities. According to John Tigrett, he did this to give him future leverage of over those he bribed. I obtained a number of these Hammer tapes after his death in 1990 from a family member.

The Hammer tapes came in formats including reels, cassettes, and micro-cassettes, which reflected the changes in recording technology from 1963 to 1981. They had been made in hotels, restaurants, cars, offices, and unknown venues. The unwitting participants included everyone from lowly employees of Occidental Petroleum to a sitting president of the United States, John F. Kennedy. Hammer taped his own Board directors, executives, lawyers, consultants, and go-betweens. He also taped himself describing his meetings with foreign leaders. In all, they contained some sixty hours of conversation—although not all the recordings were immediately audible.

Putting them in the context of Hammer's activities was no easy task. After getting these tapes, I played them for George Williamson. He had been president of Occidental in Libya when some of the tapes were made and had remained Hammer's close personal friend. Williamson had no problem recognizing Hammer's raspy voice and even recalled a few of the meetings on the tapes. Hammer's family members also recognized his voice. I next commissioned a forensic analysis that compared parts of the tapes with samples of his voice taken from his appearance on a radio program in 1979. It confirmed their authenticity. I played the tapes to several of his former secretaries, aides, or business associates none of them admitted any prior knowledge of them or about Hammer's practice of surreptitiously recording conversations. At this point, I only knew Hammer had recorded his dealings, but I didn't know why he kept this record or the identities of the people with whom he was meeting.

I found one intriguing lead. A typed note stapled to one microcassette made in July 1979 said:

> Enclosed are (1) the original microcassette of the recording made in your office on July 23 and (2) an insurance copy of the same recording on a standard cassette (which I used to make the verbatim transcript I gave you.) In keeping with the confidential nature of the recording, the labels are written in Russian. There are no other copies of either of the recordings or the transcript.

It was signed simply "JH."

I called Julian Hammer, his Russian-speaking son. Julian, his only son, readily admitted to me that he was the "JH" wgo wrote the note.

I next went to see Julian at his home in Bel-Air to discuss the tapes. Julian explained that his father assigned him this "discrete task" because he did not trust his regular employees to perform what Armand Hammer called "James Bond stuff." Taking advantage of Julian's technical skills with electronics—skills he had developed initially as a hobby—Armand Hammer had him install a sophisticated recording system in his home and office. Then, he had him devise a micro-cassette recorder that he could conceal on his person. Its miniature microphone was concealed in one of Armand Hammer's gold cufflinks. On several occasions, he would have Julian come to his private office and stand there shirtless while Julian taped the recorder to his body and ran the wires to the cufflink. As Julian rigged him up, he could also sense the power his father derived from being able to secretly tape the words of people close to him. He would watch him put on his shirt, tie, and jacket and, with the confidence this concealed weapon gave him, he went to his appointed meeting. He would then bring the cassette back to Julian, who would return to him a copy on a conventional cassette along with a transcript.

    Although Julian did not always know the identity of the voices on the tapes, he realized through transcribing the conversations that his father's cash payments were meant to advance his enterprise of building a major oil company from scratch. He knew his father was paying bribes and then secretly taping the bribees' acknowledgment of the bribes. His father also taped conversations with executives that he was about to fire and explained to Julian he always "needed an edge." He also told Julian that he employed only undocumented servants so he could fire them without fear they would complain to the authorities. Hammer gradually extended the James Bond operations by having Julian plant hidden surveillance devices in other people's homes, cars and offices. Julian knew much of what he was doing for his father was illegal but he saw he had little choice. It was the only service his father ever asked him to perform.

     One tape that Julian made in November 1971 was of particular interest to me. It was made by a concealed microphone in a desk in his Armand Hammer's home in Los Angeles. Julian said his father told him it provided valuable leverage because it concerned an ongoing crime. In listening to it, Julian realized crime involved the bribing of high officials in Venezuela. We listened together to the tape.

Hammer began the conversation, asking "You talked to the minister, didn't you?"

"Yes sir," answered the respondent in a deep southern accent. He was, as I later learned from Tigrett, John D. Askew, a native of Arkansas, who served as Hammer's "conduit and agent." Askew, who had been doing business in Venezuela since 1946, told Hammer that Venezuela was going to invite foreign oil companies to bid on developing five large tracts near Lake Maracaibo that contained an estimated three billion barrels of oil. These concessions were to take the form of "service contracts" that guaranteed the foreign companies a substantial proportion of the oil revenue for seven years. Up until then, two international oil companies, Exxon (then Esso) and Shell had a near-monopoly on oil production in Venezuela. Askew told Hammer on the tape that he could win three of the five tracts for

Occidental if he paid $3 million in cash under the table, or as Hammer said, "outside the money that is paid under the contract.

"He's getting paid isn't he?" Hammer continued.

Tigrett later explained to me that Hammer had routed the $3 million to Askew from the Worldwide Trading Corporation, Occidental's Liberian subsidiary, through a corporation called Noark International to two Panamanian shell corporations.

"You betcha," Askew answered.

"Well, then why in the hell won't he deliver?" Hammer asked, referring to the fact thar the tracts had not yet been awarded to his company, Occidental.

"This isn't such a big thing," Hammer said.

"Yes, it is to them. It's beyond their powers." Askew answered. "It's strictly political. I hate discussing this but maybe you're not paying this Minister enough."

"How much are we paying? The total amount of money."

"We've paid three million dollars," responds Askew.

"How is that three million divided?" Hammer asks. "Who gets what?"

Askew answers, "It's beyond their powers. It is strictly political."

Hammer answers, "Money talks." He tells Askew to "take a quarter of a million or even a half million of that money away from other people," and use an intermediary to "go to Caldera." (Rafael Caldera was the President of Venezuela. }

Hammer was relentless in pressing Askew for the names of those who split his bribe. Askew gradually named a dozen recipients. They were his partners in the service contract that Askew had earned through the consulting work he had performed for Occidental.

Since I could not identify many of the names in the chain of recipients, I brought the tapes to William Luers who, before becoming president of the Metropolitan Museum of Art in New York. Had been the U.S. ambassador to Venezuela.

When I began playing the cassette for Luers in his office at the Met, his demeanor changed. He took notes and he seemed particularly interested in a portion that concerned "Pedro." In it, Hammer asks who is being paid off:

"One million is divided to Pedro and his bunch," Askew responds.

"That's Tinoco? He gets a million?"

"Yeah," Askew says.

Luers explained that Tinoco had been, before his death in 1992, one of the most powerful men in Caracas. Not only had Tinoco been the minister of finance but his father had served as minister of the interior in a dictatorship. Luers described Tinoco as a heavy man with a square face and a bald head, whose law firm specialized in international business. He also owned one of Venezuela's leading banks, the Banco Latino. After serving as finance minister, he went on to become head of Venezuela's central bank. In this latter role, Luers said he worked with the U.S. government and was considered, "America's man in Caracas."

Hammer described him on the tape as "a tough guy [who] could go in and see the president."

"My guess is that when this becomes public, they will try to hang the whole thing on Tinoco since he is dead," Luers said. "Do you really want to open this Pandora's box?"

I next went to see the Venezuelan ambassador to the United Nations, Enrique Tejera. I understood that Ambassador Tejera, who had served as foreign minister, was a close friend of President Caldera. As I prepared to play the tape in his office, he joked, "I hope I'm not on the tape."

He told me on his first meeting with Hammer in Caracas in 1969, Hammer had insisted on showing him a videotape of a ceremony in which he stood with King Idris of Libya. Tejara assumed that it was Hammer's way of making the point that he had obtained his oil concession in Libya through his connections to the king. Hammer had also, as I knew, delivered a multimillion-dollar payoff to one of Idris's inner circle.

"Venezuela is not Libya," Tejara said. "We take corruption very seriously. We have had strictly enforced anti-bribery laws since 1936 and we have put two presidents in prison for it."

I played the tape. It took about twenty minutes. When it concluded, he walked to his desk and placed a call to President Caldera. A few moments later, Caldera called him back and, in my presence, he described in Spanish the contents of the tape. Caldera then asked for a transcript, which I agreed to supply.

After the president hung up, Ambassador Tejera placed a call to Maurice Vallery, who, in 1971, had headed the Venezuelan National Petroleum Company (CVP), which had awarded Occidental the three service contracts. He reached him in Caracas on his cellular phone and, after summarizing the situation, handed me the telephone.

On the tape, Askew, in accounting for the disbursement of the $3 million in cash, explains:

"Then I come back and had to give to Vallery. I swung him a half a million dollars. I gave him $250,000 and he said; 'Now I'm going to work this out.' I said O.K. He said he got some other people in with him . . ."

"You gave Vallery a half million," Hammer summed up.

"He is a 100 percent with us . . ." Askew answered.

I repeated this portion of the tape to Vallery.

"Voices from the grave," he said. He expressed shock that Hammer could have talked about him in this way. "I had little to do with Hammer. I saw him at the ceremony in which the contracts were signed and I had dinner with him once and he told me about his meeting with Lenin. The only thing he ever gave me was a catalog for his art collection." As for Askew, he recalled meeting him only once at a large social function.

I asked about the putative half-million-dollar payoff. "That's pure invention," he answered. "Probably Askew cheated Hammer out of the money."

Tigrett scoffed at this explanation. "The Venezuelans are just covering their asses," he said. "No one cheated Hammer and survived." And, in fact, Hammer got the concessions.

I recalled a plaque in Hammer's office that described his personal Golden Rule as "He who hath the gold makes the rules." His recording showed that Hammer applied it to build an oil empire by using his gold to bribe government officials to give him the concessions he needed.

PART THREE

HAMMER'S DEATH MARCH

On November 25 1990, Armand Hammer readied himself for the black-tie dinner celebrating the opening of an institution that he had erected in marble-- the Armand Hammer Museum of Art and Cultural Center. He knew from the grim prognosis he had recently received from his doctors that this might be his last public appearance. He was 92 years old and suffered from chronic anemia, bronchitis, prostate enlargement, kidney ailments and an irregular heartbeat and cancer that was rapidly spreading throughout his body. He also ever more frequently lost contact with reality and hallucinated. His night nurse, who twice earlier that fall had used artificial respiration to revive him, had now been instructed not to intervene again. But even in a weakened condition, he was determined to attend this event.

He had had a massive blood transfusion, which made his mind more acute. He also had a large dosage of analgesics, which relieved the pain in his body. He had his hair trimmed and was fitted with a new tuxedo designed to conceal his recent weight-loss. He was then strapped into his wheel-chair and, barely conscious when he was carried down the steps of his home in the Westwood section of Los Angeles to the waiting limousine.

Up until 1987, he had planned to leave his priceless art collection to the Los Angeles County Museum of Art. His plan was to immortalize his name by creating a virtual museum within a museum for his collection. But when he revised his terms for the gift that year and demanded that that part of the museum, the Armand Hammer wing, would be run by a curator that was appointed in perpetuity by him or his designated agent, the Armand Hammer Foundation, its Board of Trustees refused to acquiesce to that extraordinary arraignment. He then revoked his pledge gift and proceeded to build a museum inside the Occidental building that he could control posthumously through his foundation.

Although it would cost over eighty million dollars, he relied on Occidental Petroleum Corporation to provide the financing. He had built this company from a near-bankrupt corporate shell in 1955 to the fourteenth largest industrial company in the U.S. Though he owned less than one percent of its stock, he was chairman and could count on it to do his bidding. He had often used its corporate treasury to fund his art acquisition as, for example, when he had it secretly donate the $6 million to his foundation in 1980 that he used to buy the celebrated Leonardo da Vinci notebook, which he then renamed the Hammer Codex and exhibited around the world. I had flown with him to London to pick it up. He now wanted a special hall in the new museum dedicated to the Hammer Codex. He also wanted the museum erected adjacent to Occidental's headquarters on Wilshire Boulevard, with its outer walls build of white marble imported from the same quarry in Italy that Da Vinci had used five centuries earlier and his name carved in letters three feet high on two sides of the museum.

Occidental accommodated him by donating to the museum the real estate its corporate headquarters stood on (and then leasing back its office building) and constructing the edifice according to Hammer's approved design. It also provided Hammer's museum with a $36 million endowment that would be used to subsidize its operating expenses. Even though some Occidental shareholders had sued the company over the expenditures it had made on this enterprise, which *Newsweek* described it disparagingly as "more like a mausoleum than a museum,"

Hammer was not deterred. He was determined to open it on schedule.
He had assembled that night at the Armand Hammer Museum the leading lights of Los Angeles society. He now enjoyed the status not just of a captain of industry but of a world celebrity. He could claim to have been received by no fewer than eight American Presidents in the White House and by almost as many Soviet Presidents, as well as Lenin himself, in the Kremlin. His international awards included the Soviet Union's Order of Friendship, America's National Medal of the Arts, France's Legion of Honor, Italy's Grand Order of Merit, Sweden's Royal Order of the Polar Star, Austria's Knight Commander's Cross, Pakistan's Hall-I-Quad.-Adam Peace Award, Israel's Leadership Award, Venezuela's Order of Andres Bello, Mexico's National Recognition Award, Bulgaria's Jubilee Medal and Belgium's Commander of the Order of the Crown. He even had a school, the Armand Hammer World College, named in his honor.

Though still woozy from drugs and blood transfusions, he greeted the long parade of acquaintances. They included the executives at Occidental, who were waiting to take over from him, the art curators, who had authenticated his paintings for decades, the politicians, whom he had helped finance, the doctors, who could do little further for him, the lawyers, ready to litigate his estate and his surviving family-- his only son, Julian, 61 years ago, and his grandson, Michael, the executor of his estate, and granddaughter, Casey.

After cutting the ceremonial ribbon, he took his seat at the table of honor. On his right, was Danielle Mitterand, the wife of the President of France. She had agreed to come to the opening after he had pledged a $300,000 donation to President Mitterand's private foundation in France. He had learned over five decades that bribing famous people, even in the guise of a donation to their foundation, was the most expedient way to get them to attend his self-glorifying events. Across from him was Tom Bradley, the Mayor of Los Angeles, whose re-election campaign he had generously supported and Rabbi Harvey Fields, who was helping him organize an extraordinary bar mitsvah ceremony that was scheduled to take place in two weeks. Although Hammer had never had the traditional bar mitsvah at the age of 13, and denied his Jewish heritage most of his life, he now wanted at his advance age to undergo this rite of passage. On his left was Hilary Gibson, a white-haired women with striking features, and a secret that only she and Hammer shared.

Hilary Gibson had played an instrumental role in creating the museum. Grasping her hand under the table, Hammer said "We did it." It was the culmination of a 17 yearlong secret relationship in which she was, as she would put it, his "confidante, friend, business associate, co-habitant, consultant, nurse, mistress and lover." He had been her King Pygmalion, transforming her over these years into a totally new identity. When she had met Hammer in August 1974, her name was not Hilary Gibson; it was Martha Wade Kaufman. She was then an exceedingly comely 38 years old woman with flaming red hair. She was married to a USC professor and the mother of two young daughters. She had come to California from Ohio as an airline stewardess but then earned a degree in fine art at California State University. She had decided to try her hand at art journalism and Hammer was her first assignment. East-West Publications, which publishes magazines for airlines, had commissioned her to write about Hammer's art collection and Occidental's public relations department had arranged for her to meet Hammer at 9 a.m. in his office that day. But, when she arrived that morning, he was not there. She elected to wait by sitting in a cubicle outside his door most of the day. When he finally arrived at five in the afternoon, he profusely apologized for the eight-hour delay and ordered his secretary to bring them both ice teas. He was heavier than she expected (he weighed almost 206 pounds) but walked with a robust spring in his step. She noticed that he was dressed in an immaculately tailored gray suit, a white shirt and an elegant tie. He also had a deep tan that set off his lucid eyes. He looked remarkably vigorous for a man she knew was in his late seventies.

She watched him assess her carefully. He later would tell her "You didn't stand a chance." She began the interview trying to be as professional as possible. She asked him his motive for collecting art and whether he considered it another business investment or a profound passion.
Instead of answering her questions, he abruptly changed the subject to a painting in his collection. He showed it to her in the catalogue of his private collection. "It could be you," he said looking at her with a fixed gaze. He then explained that the artist's mistress was the model for that painting and told her that her colors perfectly matched the flesh tones in the painting. He then looked at his watch and told her he had an appointment with his barber and asked her if she minded continuing the interview while he was getting his hair cut.
She had little choice if she wanted to complete the interview. At the barber shop, instead of the discussion about art she expected, he interviewed her about her

marital status. She told him that her marriage was rocky and that she wanted more out of life than being someone's wife and that she was in the process of separating from her husband.

When his hair cut was complete--which took only a few minutes-- he had another surprise for her. He pulled her towards his waiting limousine and told they would have to complete the interview en route to the airport where his private plane was waiting to fly him to Moscow. Again, rather than discussing his collection, he preferred telling him about his unique standing in Moscow. He told her he had met Lenin and almost every other important Soviet leader. She was impressed. As they neared the airport, he guardedly scribbled a question to her on a piece of paper-- as if he was afraid his spoken words might be monitored. What was her home telephone? She answered it and, passing the paper back to him, was amazed to see him erase his original question. She was intrigued by the layer of conspiracy he had imposed on a simple request.

Hammer called her a few weeks later. In a very business-like way, he told her he was back in Los Angeles and he had thought about her questions and now wanted to complete the interview. He suggested that she meet him that afternoon at a private suite at the Beverly Hills Hilton Hotel which he used when he did not want to be disturbed by routine office business.

He opened the door for her when she arrived at the suite and seated her on a sofa across a table from him. When she took out her pad to take notes, he told her that what he was saying was not for publication but he wanted her to hear him out. She was slightly mystified by the request but put down her pad.

Speaking with almost brutal frankness, he told her about his interest in building a serious art collection. He explained that art for him was neither a business nor an aesthetic passion; it was a means to achieve an end-- immortalizing his name. He wanted to leave behind such an unrivaled collection that future generations would associate the Hammer name with greatness. To do this, he intended to spare no expense in buying renowned masterpieces. To give it prominence during his lifetime, he would exhibit the collection in the great museums of the world. After his death, it would be housed in a separate building in the Los Angeles County Museum of Art, where it would stand, forever, as a monument to him. He told her he had already made the preliminary arrangements with the Los Angeles County Museum but he still had to improve the collection and create a global reputation for it. He told her the real purpose behind this meeting: He wanted her to leave journalism and work closely with him in realizing this prodigious ambition. She would act as his personal art consultant, curator and liaison with museums around the world. She would have her own office at Occidental and travel with him on his private jet. She would help him make the arrangements for exhibiting the Armand Hammer collection around the world. He then leaned close to her, suggesting this would be more than a professional relationship, and told her he was offering her a new life. If she accepted, she would, as he put it, "never have to worry about money again."

She was overwhelmed by this sweeping proposal and the confident manner in which he had delivered it. "Why me?" she asked. He replied that he felt himself "drawn to her" from the moment they met. He said he could sense that she wanted to learn from him. "I want to take care of you," he said, embracing her like a child. He then led her to the adjoining bedroom and began the sex relationship that would change her life. After Hammer left the suite, Kaufman saw that he had left five one-hundred bills on the table for her. Insulted, she left them on the table. But his message was clear-- if crude. On September 22, 1974, she was put on the payroll of Occidental at a starting salary of $22,000 per year. She nominally worked for Occidental's public relations department, but, in reality, she could come and go as she liked, without reporting to her superior in the department. She reported directly to Hammer. The job provided a plausible reason for her meetings with Hammer in foreign countries including Venezuela,

Peru, Mexico, Britain and Japan. She also found the job extremely challenging since it involved not only arranging exhibitions for the Armand Hammer Collection but, making sure that the officials, socialites and journalists who Hammer wanted to cultivate favor with would be invited.

When Hammer traveled with his wife Francis on the corporate jet, she would take a commercial flight to the same destination. But on almost these trips, he would then find opportunities to liaise with her. In Paris, for example, he took her to a Russian restaurant, which he had closed to other customers. As they sat alone there, served by a dozen waiters and serenaded by an entire gypsy orchestra, she marveled at his power to magically empty a restaurant when it suited his purposes.

She also found that Hammer had his own golden rule: "He Who Hath The Gold, Makes The Rules." He had it inscribed on a plaque in his office, and pointing it out to her, he told her "like it or not, this is the way life is." She soon found out how serious he was about imposing his rules on her. When, for example, she sought a legal divorce from his husband in 1976, he told her not to seek either alimony or child support for her daughters from him. If she did, he explained to her that her husband might retaliate by exposing her relationship with him and he could not risk having his name surface. Instead, he asked her to arrange an uncontested divorce and he would provide her and her daughters with lifetime support. She followed his instructions and was now heavily dependent on Hammer for her employment.

In 1978, Hammer told her that he was transferring her from Occidental to the Armand Hammer Foundation. She would serve there as his personal art consultant at a salary of $30,000. This change increased her dependence on him which she assumed was partly his motive. Instead of working for Occidental, where she might find some corporate insulation, she worked directly for him from her home in Beverly Hills-- a home he had encouraged her to buy because it had an alley that led to a back entrance, ingredients that Hammer had always found helpful in maintaining a double life. Having his limousine driver bring him to this alley, he could keep his visits discreet. It was to be his private retreat. He had her decorate it like an English cottage with furniture that had belonged to his deceased brother, Harry. In the master bedroom was an "Adjuster" bed, so he could raise and lower in different positions, and mirrors on the wall, so he could watch himself perform . In the garden, he had her plant his favorite flower, double-delight roses that changed from white to deep red.

Usually, he would arrive about noon time take off the tie and jacket he wore to the office and make himself comfortable at the table in the kitchen. She found he liked to make phone calls in her presence to the White House, Kremlin, Buckingham Palace and other centers of power, as if to impress her. When speaking to lesser people, she noticed he would almost always dispense with the usual polite "hellos" and "good-byes. He would tersely state his business and hang up. After lunch, he would often put on a robe and sun himself in the garden. He would tell her during these visits, "You make me young." And she did what she could to restore his youth, putting him on the low-fat Dr. Atkins diet (his weight dropped from 206 when she first met him to 165 pounds) and helping him "think young." Aside from her salary, he had promised her a lifetime income after his death that was to be paid out of a secret bank account in Switzerland. Since he was not in the best of health, and an octogenarian, this Swiss Account was an important part of their deal. It was not an easy bargain for her. He demanded an extraordinary measure of control over her personal life during the course of the next 12 years. She had to be available to meet his schedule at short notice. He gave her two beepers to alert her to his calls. He prohibited her from seeing other men and, to make sure of her whereabouts in Los Angeles, he had a homing device installed in her car and a tap placed on her phone. He also frequently had her wear a disguise when they were together in public so she would not be recognized. He also controlled her vacation schedule-- for example, making sure she came to New York when he had to be there overnight on business (He maintained a town house in Greenwich Village there that he used for these meetings.) She had to submit to his sexual demands even when she considered them, as she later described them to me, as "extremely humiliating." She also accommodated him by mirroring her bedroom when he told her he enjoyed watching himself. Despite his advanced age, she found him to be physically energetic, which he attributed to swimming laps every day in his home indoor pool.

He went far beyond any conventional romantic liaison by attempting to extend his domain to her reproductive organs. Hammer wanted her to bear him an illegitimate son. He would not take no for an answer, but, though he kept careful track of her menstrual cycle, she did not get pregnant. He then forced her, as she later described it, "to undergo surgical procedures to facilitate impregnation"-procedures he had "conducted under his direct view and direction." They also failed.

When Hammer decided to build his own museum, he involved her in the project, raising her salary to $70,000 in 1989. But Francis found out that she was Hammer's mistress. She had previously suspected a liaison, but Hammer had managed to persuade her that she was mistaken. Now, even though he again denied the truth, she was not convinced. Since Francis' own fortune, which she inherited before he married her in 1955, had helped finance the art collection, he needed her cooperation in transferring the art to the museum and could not risk her impeding the project. Nor did he want to give up his mistress, as she demanded. He therefore designed an ingenious ploy to dupe his wife.

After telling her that he had fired his Martha Kaufman from the foundation, he had his mistress assume a new identity under the name of "Hilary Gibson." He then told Francis that he had hired "Gibson" as a replacement for Kaufman. To further diminish her suspicion, he had his mistress transform herself into a much elderly woman, telling her that older woman pass unnoticed at social functions. He made her, as she later noted, "wear wigs, glasses, make-up and attire which made her appear decades older than she really was." When he was satisfied with his make-over, he re-employed her both at the Foundation and

Occidental, where she had to disguise "her true identity from co-workers." She recalled that he took immense pleasure in the success of this deception.

Francis died that December. But by this time the persona of Hilary Gibson was well established. She was the director of planning, development and financial control for the museum-- a position from which she personally supervised all aspects of this creation of Hammer's monument. She even oversaw the engraving in marble of the letters of his name. By the fall, Hammer's visits to her home became less frequent, and she put all her energies into making sure of the success of the grand opening. She also drew up a new contract for herself that gave her lifetime remuneration from the foundation, and, a week before the opening, Hammer had signed it.

The opening ended abruptly for Hammer at 10 p.m. when two medical attendants picked him, like a rag doll, and carried him out. When he got home that night, he had a prolonged hallucination. He saw his dead mother in the room and, in front of his staff, he carried on a rambling conversation with her, asking her over and over again where his missing father was. His night nurse could not convince him that it was only a hallucination. The next week, two faith-healers were brought in. They floated Hammer on the surface of the swimming pool and, in a repetition of an ancient Aztec ceremony, they danced around him for two days. On 7.22 p.m., on December 10, Hammer died in bed-- it was the night before his scheduled Bar Mitzvah. About an hour later, Michael Armand Hammer, Hammer's 32-year old grandson, arrived at the house. He had just returned in his new Ferrari from a weekend balloon festival in Palm Springs. He sorted through his grandfather's personal effects and gave away or took Hammer's gold Rolex watch, a tie clip, and a bottle of Dom Perignon champagne. Meanwhile, the Occidental security men loaded cartons of Hammer's papers into a van in the driveway. Before they could leave, they were blocked by Richard Cleary, the lawyer representing Frances Hammer's estate. He said that since Hammer's home had reverted to his wife's estate the moment Hammer died, they had no right to remove anything from the house without the estate's permission. He called in the Los Angeles police while the security men called Michael out to the driveway. The standoff continued until about 1:30 a.m. Finally, Stafford Matthews, Hammer's lawyer, arrived and worked out an agreement whereby all the cartons were returned to a locked room in the house, to which Michael retained the key. Cleary then had an all-night locksmith change the front door locks, effectively evicting Michael. The reports on the police radio about the confrontation in the street alerted the night editors at the *Los Angeles Times* to Hammer's death. His obituary, drawn from a clip file that spanned nearly seven decades, had already been prepared. At 6:00 a.m., it sent out news over its wire service of his death. Nevertheless, his bar mitzvah went on as planned without him.

The attendees at the funeral two days later got another surprise when a born-again pastor stood up and announced that on his deathbed Hammer had renounced his newly embraced Jewish heritage and "accepted Jesus Christ as his savior." The man who announced Hammer's deathbed conversion at the funeral was Douglas L. Mobley, the father of Michael Hammer's wife, Dru Ann Mobley.

The memorial service took place at the Museum on January 4, 1991. Hilary Gibson stood alone in the row immediately behind the Occidental Board of Directors. She was feleing very much like, as she put it, "a pariah." Even since the funeral, the new management at Occidental had begun to distance itself from Hammer. His pet projects, such as Armand Hammer Film Productions, had been terminated. His photographs, paintings and busts taken down. The framed letters and testimonials to Hammer from world leaders also had been removed from the sixteenth floor executive suite. She could see "the handwriting on the wall" for herself. She had been Hammer's mistress for 17 years and the museum, which Hammer had meant her to run, had become the subject of a huge shareholders suit. She knew the new management was moving to distance itself from both her and the museum. The Leonardo De Vinci book, which he had named the Hammer Codex, would be sold to William Gates of Microsoft-and re-named The Gates Codex. The museum would be turned over to UCLA to manage. She would be put through, as she termed it, "total hell." Throughout the following months she found herself progressively more isolated. Her title was revoked and, finally, on June 2, 1992 two Occidental security men escorted her out of the building. She was fired.

The foundation had also dispensed with her services and made it clear to her that to settle her claim against it, she would have to sue it.

She also received no money from the secret fund he had told her he had set up for her in Switzerland. He had led her to believe it contained at least 10 million dollars-- and that this was money he had diverted from oil deals he had made in Libya. Yet, when she asked lawyers for Hammer's estate about it, they denied it existed.

What these lawyers did not anticipate was her extraordinary determination-- and resourcefulness. "If I could handle Hammer for 17 years, I could handle anything." she later reflected. She had made copies of numerous addresses she found on papers in his pocket during Hammer's visits to her home. Even though he often used code-names, she was able to identify a key Swiss banker-- Felix Iselin. In 1994, she flew to Basel and arranged a meeting with Iselin at his office.

Iselin was very brusque and business-like. He told her that Hammer he made arraignments for her but revoked them. He then took a hand-written document from his file. It was addressed to Peter Lotz, one of his partners and dated September 6, 1990. She could see that most of the words on it had been meticulously blocked out with masking tape for her viewing. The unblocked portion read: "My instructions with regard to ... Martha Kaufman (Hilary Gibson) are revoked." It was signed "Armand Hammer." Iselin looked at her smugly, as if that ended the issue.

She then calculatingly asked Iselin for some information. When he left to get it for her, she grabbed the document and, concealing it under her shawl, calmly left the office. By the time she had arrived at her hotel, there was a frantic message from Iselin, begging her to return the document. Instead, she peeled off the masking tape and found the name of the secret account-- the Grazioza Account– that Hammer had established for her. The full document also showed that Hammer had secreted money outside of the U.S. that he did not intend to pass through his estate-- or pay taxes on. She speculated that this disclosure could prove enormously embarrassing to the estate. She now also knew that her lover had double-crossed her a few months before he died by revoking his commitment. She decided to sue his estate for his breach of promise.

Confronted with the document, the lawyers representing Hammer's estate, living trust and Occident settled her claim out of court. In March 1996, she received $4.2 million. She had finally challenged Hammer's Golden Rule—and won.

PART FOUR
THE HAMMER SUCCESSION

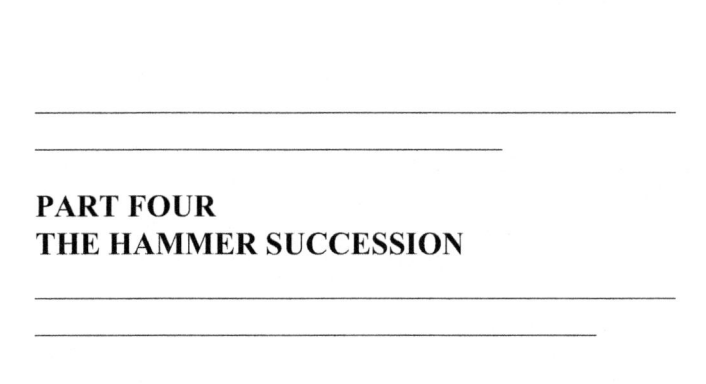

[1]
The Patriarch: Julius Hammer

Julius Hammer stood in manacles and leg irons on September 18, 1920. He was now prisoner 71516 in Sing Sing penitentiary, described in the prison blotter as "46 years old, 5 foot 11 inches tall, 195 pounds, Hebrew religion." But these brief prison notations hardy described one the man who before his imprisonment was one of the most extraordinary political figures in America.

He came to the United States in 1875 at the age of 16 from a Jewish Ghetto in Odessa, which was then part of the Russian Empire. Since his father already had obtained American citizen, he automatically became an American citizen. He first worked in a foundry where he became a fiercely anti-capitalist socialist. By the time, he was 18, he was a leading member of the radical Socialist Labor Party, whose motto was "Down with the political state, up with the industrial state." Its leader was Daniel De Leon, a dedicated Marxist who advocated civil war in America. With Hammer's help, the party would evolve into the U.S. Communist Party.

In 1897, Julius, settled in the Bronx, married Rose Lipshitz, who had a son, Harry, by a previous marriage. Julius gave Harry his last name. In May of the following year, Julius had his own son, who he named Armand Hammer after the arm-and-hammer insignia of the Socialist Labor Party.

He also ran a lucrative chain of five drugstores, went to medical school and opened up a medical practice in his home. When the Socialist Labor Party ran short of money, he used the profits from his drug stores to finance it.

After a spate of anarchist bombings in the early 1900s, Hammer and his associates were pursued by the Red Squad of the New York police. After sending his wife and children to live with friends, Hammer went to Europe to attend the meeting of the Second International in Stuttgart, Germany. There be met Lenin, who recruited him into his underground cadre that was planning to start a world revolution.

   Hammer returned to the United States as a dedicated agent of Lenin. When Lenin seized power in Russia in November 1917, the U.S. imposed an embargo against Russia in order to strangle Lenin's Communist regime in its crib. America and allies might have succeeded if not for Julius Hammer. He became the Commercial Attaché of the "Soviet Government Bureau" that Lenin set up in New York. Along with Ludwig Martens, Lenin's unofficial and unrecognized "ambassador" to the U.S., Hammer funded the operations of Soviet Government Bureau by laundering the proceeds from the illegal sales of Russian smuggled diamonds . He also set up the Allied Drugs and Chemical company as a front to smuggle materials into Soviet Russia, including farm equipment, medicine, and the spare parts that Lenin desperately needed to keep alive his revolutionary government.Through his crucial role in smuggling supplies into Russia, Hammer came to the attention of the Justice Department and J. Edgar Hoover. Hoover decided to use Hammer and Martens embargo-busting to help justify the creation of the investigative bureau that would become the FBI under his leadership.

Hoover staged a Federal raid of the Soviet Russian Government Bureau on June 12, 1919 that missed Hammer and drove Martens into hiding. When Martens was finally captured, he was deported to Soviet Union. This left Hammer as the principal target of J. Edgar Hoover.

The government's surveillance of the Hammer house paid off on July 5, 1919, when federal agents witnessed Marie Oganesoff, the wife of a former Russian, diplomat enter Julius's medical office in his Bronx home, and learned that she received an abortion. When Oganesoff died six days later, the Feds informed the Bronx prosecutor. A Bronx County grand jury then indicted Julius Hammer for first-degree manslaughter. He was convicted and sentenced to three and a half years in Sing Sing prison. This interruption in his life presented a problem for his associates on Moscow. So Hammer, needing to replace himself, turned to his eldest son, Armand.

[2]
The Prodigal Son: Armand Hammer

Armand Hammer, born May 21, 1898 in the Bronx, was a medical student at Columbia at the time of his father's arrest. He had spent much of his childhood, along with his younger brother Victor and stepbrother Harry, being shuffled between strangers homes, as his father traveled in America and abroad, to pursue his conspiratorial aim of bringing about the revolution. He was waiting for his medical internship to begin when his father asked him to go in his place to Moscow. According to his longtime mistress and confidant Bettye Murphy, he had no real choice but to accept because he felt that he was responsible for his father's imprisonment. He told her that he often worked in his father's clinic and performed procedures when his father had to attend to his political activities. And it was he, not his father, who performed the abortion on Marie Oganesoff that proved fatal. Because he was not yet a licensed doctor, he faced certain prison. To save him, his father, who was a licensed doctor, took the blame. He wasn't concerned about prison because he wrongly assuming that as a doctor, claiming that the abortion was necessary to save the woman's life, he would escape punishment. Indeed few in any doctors had gone to prison for an abortion in the early twentieth century. But these doctors were not conduits for the Soviet government. Years after his father was convicted, Armand Hammer told Bettye that his guilt was such that he had to go to Moscow in his stead even though it meant giving up his planned medical career. Whether or not he was telling the truth about killing Oganesoff, is not known.

On July 5, 1921, Hammer boarded the S.S. Aquitania en route to Russia. After being detained briefly in England because J. Edgar Hoover, who was to be his nemesis for the next five decades, had alerted Scotland Yard that he might be carrying secret documents to Russia, he proceeded via a circuitous route through six countries to Russia. In Moscow, he met with both Martens and Lenin.

For most of the next decade, he remained mostly in Moscow. Since the business of evading Western embargoes required false documents, numbered bank accounts, money laundering and the evasion of laws in multiple countries, it afforded him the experience he needed to perfect techniques in stealth transactions, bribery and deception. To help finance his operations, the Soviet Russia government awarded him and his family some legitimate concessions including stationery supplies, asbestos mining and pencil manufacturing.

While in Russia Armand got married in 1927 to Olga Vadimovna Von Root, a Russian actress and gypsy singer, who gave birth to his first and only son. He named him Julian Armand Hammer,.

Whether it was he, his father or his covert Russians associates ,who decided that The Hammers needed an American base of operations for laundering Russian art and other goods, he moved back to New York in 1930.

After his return, he ran perhaps the largest art laundering scheme in history. The Soviet regime, which had expropriated and plundered a vast amount of art from Russian citizens and museums, could not openly sell it on the open market in America without risking lawsuits from its previous owners, yet it desperately needed the hard currency this art could produce to fund its secret operations abroad. The solution it found was to have Hammer provide a fake provenance for it by pretending the art came from his own private collection he had amassed during his ten years in Russia. He could then sell the pieces without raising ownership questions. Since it actually came from the Russian government, he secretly remitted the money to Russia, less his commission, through the device of fake purchases for wood and other commodities from Amtorg, the Soviet trading company. Over the next nine years, Russia shipped literally trainloads of art objects, some of which it recently manufactured and forged, to Hammer in New York. Hammer, always enterprising, found ways to sell it through department store and art galleries. To give him plausible cover for the art and his other under-the table activities during his ten years in Russia, he needed a plausible cover story or, as it called by intelligence services, a legend. Walter Duranty, the *New York Times* correspondent in Moscow, ghostwrote it for him in the form of an autobiographical memoir called *The Quest for the Romanoff Treasures*. Duranty, a short man who hobbled around Moscow on a wooden leg, was sympathetic to the Soviet regime, and provided Hammer with an elegantly-written legend which both concealed his work for the regime and provided him a story portraying him as a wily art collecting and capitalist. Since the truth about his covert activities would not be known until after the KGB archives became available in 1992, he could satisfy suspicions of art buyers, businessmen, or other people had about his time in Russia by gifting them a copy of *The Quest for the Romanoff Treasures*. He sent signed copy of the book to every American President from Franklin Delano Roosevelt to Ronald Reagan.

But his Russian wife and son did not fit in with the Capitalist image he needed to establish. He therefore distanced himself from that part of his past initially by delaying them from joining him in America and then by physically separating himself from them by sending them to live separately from him in upstate New York and Los Angeles. He made the de facto separation into a legal one in 1943 by divorcing Olga and providing her and Julian with a $75 a week in alimony. Once his divorce was final, he married Angela Zevela, a socially-respectable opera singer.

Hammer enjoyed having a secret as well as a public life. While still married to Angela, he installed twenty-nine years old Bettye Murphy in an apartment in New York as his mistress. He had first met Bettye in April 1953 where she had been working as the manager-hostess of Laney's Supper Club at the yacht basin at Marathon, Florida. As she told me the story, Hammer beckoned her over to his table and introduced himself only as "Doc." He told her that she bore an uncanny resemblance to a girl he had known a long time ago named Marjorie who had been his one and only true love. Hammer said he met Marjorie just after he had graduated from medical school in 1921. He then found out that she had contracted tuberculosis. To cure her, he tried to get her into a sanatorium but before he could get her admitted. his father sent him to Russia and Marjorie had died.

He then asked Bettye the date of her birth. When she replied December 2, 1923, he told her that Marjorie had died just a few days before Bettye was born and that, because of their physical likeness, he believed Marjorie's life spirit may have migrated to her when she was born. When he ask her about the location of birthmarks on her body, Bettye, though sightly taken aback by the personal nature of the stranger's curiosity, was taken in by the power of his story. She accepted his invitation to go with him to Cuba and they flew there in his private Beechcraft twin-engine plane and stayed in the bridal suite of the El Presidente Hotel in Havana. When she asked about his business, he told her he was in the whisky business, which was true.

After she became his mistress, he promised her that they would get married as soon as he divorced Angela. While waiting in 1956, she became pregnant with his child. He tried to persuade her to have an abortion, even arranging a ruse by which a doctor could perform it in New York, but she refused. To keep the child a secret, he used what she termed "mental blackmail." He told her, for example, that he would hire a man to falsely claim he had sex with her and he, not Hammer, was the father. Under such pressure, he persuaded her to move to Mexico City to have the child where he arranged a fake marriage with a Mexican husband he hired for the ceremony. By doing so, he assured that his daughter, who Bettye named Victoria, would not have his surname.

While Bettye was in Mexico, Hammer obtained his divorce from Angela, and, six days later, Hammer remarried. But his new bride was not Bettye Murphy, it was Frances Barrett Tolman, a 54-year old widow who had inherited about $15 million from her late Husband Elmer Tolman. Hammer, he needed Frances' fortune to go into the oil business. And he did.

In 1957, using Frances' money, Hammer bought a controlling interest in Occidental Petroleum, a small and barely profitable oil driller based in Los Angeles. Hammer had a higher ambition for it. He planned to turn it into an international oil company, even though that meant competing with the seven giant companies, including Esso (now Exxon), Mobil, Royal Dutch Shell, Standard Oil of California, Texaco, Gulf and Anglo-Iranian Oil (now BP). These companies, known as the Seven Sisters, controlled most of the global oil market. To challenge them, he needed to acquire a concession from a government in the Middle East. Even though the Seven Sister cartel had made deals with most of the Arab governments in the Middle East for the rights to their oil, he saw an opportunity in

Libya, where its sovereign, King Idris, had not yet awarded concessions for recent discoveries. So Hammer decided to bribe Omar Shelhi, a top advisor to King Idris. He believed that bribery, an art he had honed while working for the Russians, would give him the edge he needed in Libya. After several false starts, he finally arranged a meeting with Shelhi in the Konigsberg Hotel in Bonn, Germany in 1965.

Hammer was a man who came right to the point, as Shelhi told me when I interviewed him in 1995 in Geneva. He described how Hammer took out a pad and pencil, handed it to him, and asked him to write down a number. He wanted Shelhi to name his price. Shelhi hesitated but Hammer convinced by telling him that if he cooperated he would make him "the richest man in Europe." Rather than just the usual suitcase of hundred dollars bills, Hammer offered to pay him and his associates a three percent royalty from the sale of all the oil and put it in a Swiss bank account for him. Shelhi was persuaded and, even though

Occidental had not been previously been in the running for a concession with the Libyan authorities, it got two giant concessions. Hammer was now a player in the international oil game.

The 1969 coup in Libya by Colonel Qaddafi did not change his situation since, as John Tigrett told me, Hammer simply moved the bribe from Shelhi and his associates to Qaddafi's key oil advisors.

Next, Hammer changed the history of the twentieth century by breaking the Seven Sisters' iron rule against paying any government more than a 50 percent royalty in the form of a tax. Hammer agreed to pay Qaddafi 58 percent. As a consequence of Hammer's breach of this rule, the Persian Gulf nations—Iran, Saudi Arabia, Kuwait, and others—demanded similar terms to what Libya got. Their logic was that if Hammer could afford to pay 58 percent, so could the Seven sisters. The Seven Sisters gave in but then Qaddafi jacked up his price by by demanding another two percent increment. The Seven Sisters, now caught in this ratcheting upwards of their royalty, could no longer control what had been a fairly stable system of distributing Middle Eastern oil. After Hammer's move, Saudi Arabia, Iran, Libya, Iraq and other Middle East governments transformed their oil allotments into a political weapon, and the Sever Sister cartel became history.

   By the 1980s, Hammer expanded into coal, gas pipelines, oil shale and chemical plants and even bought the Arm & Hammer baking soda company (because it contained his name.)
Hammer presenting himself as a titan of capitalism, financed political campaigns, hired powerful senators, like Albert Gore Sr., to run his subsidiaries, paid for the causes of Prince Charles, the heir to the British thrones, and befriended Presidents. Even after he was forced to plead guilty for making an illegal Watergate contribution, he received a pardon from President George Bush. But with all his money and power, he could not defeat his own bone cancer. He died December 10, 1990 at his home in Los Angeles.

[3] The Abandoned Son: Julian Hammer

Armand Hammer's only son was born in Moscow in May 7, 1929 to Olga Vadina Von Root. He was named Julian Armand Hammer as a tribute to his father Julius and the Arm and Hammer insignia of his political cause. But Olga's pregnancy had been so unexpected that Hammer suspected that he was not the biological father—and he continued to harbor these dark suspicions until 1988, when, through having a DNA sample secretly tested at UCLA medical center, he finally determined that Julian was indeed his son. Up until then, for the first 59 years of Julian's life, Hammer doubted that he was his progeny.

Hammer's estrangement from Julian began almost immediately after the Hammer family returned to New York in 1931. Julian's mother believed Hammer was embarrassed by her and Russian origins. Whatever his reasons, he told Olga that it was better if they lived apar when Julian was just six. Hammer sent her and Julian first to live in upstate New York and then to live in Los Angeles. As Julian recalled, his father all but disappeared from his life when he was still a child. He knew he had a famous father but he rarely saw him—not even on Christmas holidays. His father did not attend his wedding to Glenna Sue Ervin in 1954. Nor did he congratulate him on the birth of his son, Michael, Armand Hammer in 1955.

On the night of Julian's twenty-sixth birthday in May 1955, an event happened that temporarily brought his father back into his life. Julian killed a man.

What had happened was that Julian had invited a friend named Bruce Whitlock over to his apartment that night, and after they both drank heavily, Whitlock made sexual advances toward Julian's wife. Julian, getting his pistol from a drawer in the next room, returned and shot Whitlock to death. After the police arrested Julian for the shooting, the *Los Angeles Times*' headline, above the story about the killing, read "MILLIONAIRE'S SON KILLS GI."

Whether he liked it or not, Hammer was again linked to his son. The publicity could not have come at a worse time for Hammer. He had just divorced his second wife, Angela, and was having financial problems with his art business, the Hammer Galleries. As he needed to avoid a trial that could further embarrass him, he borrowed $50,000 in cash from Frances Barrett Tolman, who would become the third Mrs. Armand Hammer the following year. According to Julian, Hammer had a woman friend deliver the money for a bribe to a lawyer in Los Angeles. As a result of the bribe, Julian was released from jail and the state's attorney accepted his explanation that he had shot his guest in self-defense. (Hammer's wife, who witnessed the shooting, later said the shooting was cold blooded murder.)

Julian's account jibes with that of what Bettye Murphy, who was Hammer's mistress at the time of the shooting, told me. She recalled that Hammer was called at her apartment in New York and told about the shooting. After cursing Julian, Hammer swung into action. He made a series of phone calls and then gave her a sealed envelope containing $50,000.00 . As instructed, she took a commercial flight from New York to Los Angeles and delivered the envelope to a man who met her at the airport. She then took the next flight back to New York..

    Julian later wrote a letter further explaining:
"When I met Whitlock in West Virginia, I was studying journalism at Marshall College. Whitlock and I had a good time gambling and drinking. I guess I was seduced by his carefree lifestyle. He seemed to break the rules and somehow get away with it. When I shot Whitlock he was advancing towards me with a broken bottle. In fact the case never went to trial as it was dismissed following the submission made on my behalf by [Armand Hammer's lawyer]." He added, "My case may have been dismissed through the intervention of Senator Styles Bridges.".

    Whoever intervened, if his wife is to be believed, Julian got away with murder. Even though all charges against Julian were dismissed and he was free in the eyes of the law, his father would not let him forget his $50,000 bribe. He wanted his son to repay his debt to him by disappearing from public sight so that he caused him no further embarrassment. He would provide him with a cash remittance each month.

After that incident, Hammer's only service to his father was to wire him up to record his bribes. Asides for this "James Bond stuff," as Armand Hammer called it, he saw himself as an unwanted child.

When Armand Hammer died in 1990, he left a $40 million dollar estate but only left Julian, his only son, only $250,000. Julian felt so betrayed by his father that he did not attend his funeral.

   Julian died alone April 3, 1996. He was interred next to his father in the Hammer family mausoleum in the Westwood Memorial Park Cemetery, allowing him to achieve the proximity the proximity in death to his famous father that he never achieved in life.

[4]

The Chosen Successor: Michael Hammer

When Armand Hammer's final will and testimony was read in his lawyer's office on December 11, 1990, it was revealed that Hammer had bypassed his only son and made his 45-year old grandson Michael his principle heir. Michael would be executor of his estate and president of the Armand Hammer Foundation, which would receive the lion's share of what remained of his fortune. He would also collect his "golden casket" payments from Occidental, run his Armand Hammer Museum and administer his art gallery business. To be sure, Hammer had changed his will in the final months of his life. One reason was to hide aspects of his life that might emerge from discovery during the pending $440 million lawsuit filed by Joan Weiss, the heir to his late wife Frances' estate. Weiss was asserting that Hammer had systematically deceived his wife to gain sole ownership of their art collection. To hide these deceptions, he h ad entirely cut out of his will any bequest or even mention of Victoria, the out-of-wedlock daughter he had with Bettye Murphy, and, despite years of promises to take care of her, he deleted any bequest to his mistress, Martha Kaufman.

Hammer had earlier expressed doubts about Michael's ability to focus, telling his assistant Cathy Kosak, "He [Michael] can't just be generally involved with the Foundation; I have to give him a job. But Christ, Cathy, you know he is an idiot... Cathy go buy a cat, That can be Michael's job. He can watch the cat.' But now, as he faced imminent death, he decided that Michael had to be entrusted with preserving his legacy.

Michael Armand Hammer was born to Julius and Glenna Sue Hammer on September 8, 1955 in Los Angeles. Unlike his father, grandfather and great grandfather, he had no Russian connection in his past. He attended the University of San Diego, graduating with a degree in business administration, and then, at Armand Hammer's insistence, got a graduate degree at New York University's Stern School of Business in 1982. Now that he had obtained this credential, Armand Hammer arranged for him to work in Occidental Petroleum and, after three years shuffling between the company's offices, Hammer moved him to the corporation's headquarters in Los Angeles and gave him title of vice president and also appointed him to the Board of Directors.

While Michael was being groomed for business by his grandfather he met Dru Ann Mobley of Tulsa, Oklahoma, the daughter of a fiery Baptist evangelist who was working as a loan officer in a bank. According to Michael's son, "My dad was supposed to be on a flight, went to the airport, and got hammered and passed out…He missed his flight, woke up, rebooked, switched seats due to claustrophobia, and wound up next to Dru." They married on January 12, 1985 at the First Methodist Church in Tulsa.

The issue of how well Armand Hammer had groomed his successor arose in 1992 when Michael resigned from his position at Occidental. AS the sole executor for the estate and the Armand Hammer Foundation, its main asset, he allowed its funds to dwindle down to less than seven million dollars, and even amount was being sapped away by legal fees for more than a hundred claims and lawsuits. The National Symphony Orchestra wanted the balance on $250,000 that Armand Hammer had promised it for playing "Happy Birthday" at Hammer's 90th birthday celebration at the Kennedy Center;,the Danielle Mitterrand Fund wanted the $300,000 that Armand Hammer had offered the French first lady's for gracing his last public appearance at the opening of the Armand Hammer Museum and The Metropolitan Museum of Art wanted the remaining portion of the a $1.8 million that Armand Hammer had pledge in return for his name being put on its Hall of Arms and Armor on its main floor. To conserve cash Michael transferred The Armand Hammer Museum, a monument Hammer had built to himself in Occidental's headquarters, to UCLA which he gave a 99-year management agreement. He sold ammer's Leonardo Codex -- which he'd vaingloriously renamed the "Codex Hammer," and which he intended to be the centerpiece of his museum, to Bill Gates.. All that remains of Hammer's vainglorious attempt at achieving immortality, is his name on the outside of the now UCLA-run museum.

Nor did Michael do well with Hammer's venerable Knoedler Gallery, which closed down in the face of lawsuits alleging that it had sold customers about $70 million worth of forged paintings since 1994 . Knoedler had represented that these paintings were done by Jackson Pollock and other established artists but, as it turned out, they were actually painted by a forger in a garage in in Queens, New York. Michael Hammer's Knoedler was also accused of providing a false provenance for this forged art in a way not unlike the way his Armand Hammer had provided false provenances to art provided by his associates in Soviet Russia in the 1930s.

As *Vanity Fair* reported. a Knoedler accountant testified in the civil trial in 2016 that Michael Hammer had essentially used the gallery's holding company to pay for such personal expenses as a Rolls-Royce and other car and listed the proceeds from the sale of one of the cars on his W-2 as salary. Following that testimony, Knoedler reached a settlement that ended the trial.

Like his father, grandfather and great-grandfather, Michael also had problems with the criminal side of the law. In 2011, he was arrested and jailed in Santa Barbara jail for a DUI charge, but, like the homicide charge against his father, it was dropped.

Soon after Armand Hammer's will was read, Michael completely severed his relations with the other members of Armand Hammer's family, including his father Julian and sister Casey. He moved with his wife and children to the Cayman Islands and relinquished his American citizenship. But the Hammer saga did not end there.

[5]

The Movie Star: Armie Hammer

In 2011, the same year Michael Hammer was arrested in Santa Barbara, his eldest son Armie Hammer was also arrested at a United States Border Patrol checkpoint in Texas after marijuana was discovered by a sniffer dog in his car. And, like his father he spent a night in jail, where he found, as he later told an interviewer, "The inmates were great." The prosecutor dropped the charges against him. But unlike his father was a rising Hollywood star, who at that time was playing the role of Clyde Tolson, J. Edgar Hoover's sidekick, in Clint Eastwood's film *J. Edgar*. Hammer's role was not without irony since Hoover and Tolson had pursued both his great-great grandfather Julius Hammer and his great-grand father Armand Hammer for suspected subversive activities.

Armand Douglas Hammer was born on August 28, 1986, in Santa Monica, California to Dru Ann and Michael Hammer. As a child he was called Armie,

When he was seven, his family moved to the Cayman Islands. He later described it in a TV interview as "the fucking paradise" of the Cayman Islands." He also recalled in the interview that his Cayman Island home jad "a painting of Gorbachev," the former leader of the Soviet Union, who had given it to Armand Hammer.

Armie first attended Faulkner's Academy in Governor's Harbour, Cayman Islands, and then went to Grace Christian Academy, which the Hammer family had established as a ministry in West Bay, Grand Cayman. When his family moved back to L.A, he transferred to the Los Angeles Baptist High School in the San Fernando Valley but he dropped out in the eleventh grade to pursue an acting career which caused Michael Hammer to disowned him.

Armie had his breakthrough to Hollywood stardom in *The Social Network*, a film about the origins of Facebook in which he portrayed both of the Winklevoss identical twins who claimed to have created it. After that, with his quoted fee rising to 8-digits, he starred in *The Lone Ranger, The Man from U.N.C.L.E.* and *Call Me By My Name.*

As with Icarus flying too close to the sun, Armie's meteoric rise into the heights of Hollywood stardom abruptly ended in a crash. In January 2021, women tweeted and posted dark allegations claiming Hammer had sexually abused them. An anonymous Instagram account released screenshots it claimed were messages Hammer had sent to various women whom he had affairs with between 2016 and 2020, and which described his sexual fantasies including rape and cannibalism. A woman he dated in 2020 claimed he branded her by carving his initial "A" into her pelvis, and that he suggested that she have a lower rib surgically removed so he could eat it. Another woman he dated alleged g that he said he wanted to eat her flesh. And someone leaked videos from his private Instagram account in which he stated he was having sexual relations with "Miss Cayman" in the Cayman Islands—a false claim which led to an investigation by the Cayman police. Even more damaging, a woman's claim on Instagram that he had raped her in L.A, in 2017 led to an L.A. police investigation.

To be sure, his illustrious great-grandfather Armand Hammer had also been accused of sexual abuse and mind-control by his mistress. But that was in an age where there was no Instagram and social media and Armand Hammer was able to silence them. While Armie denied all the social media charges against him , and none of the investigations led to prosecutions, his promising career was over.

Karl Marx famously wrote that historical entities appear two times, "the first as tragedy, then as farce." While he was referring to Napoleon and his nephew Napoleon III, his idea also might apply to the five-generation saga of the Hammers. The story began with Julius Hammer changing world history by creating a lifeline of supplies for Lenin's embryonic revolution in Russia, followed by his son Armand subverting and forever changing the international oil market, and it ended with, and likely will be best remembered by, his great-great grandson Armie Hammer exposed in a social media-fueled sex scandal in Hollywood.

--The End--

ACKNOWLEDGMENTS

I am deeply grateful to Cynthia Anderson who was my chief researcher on the project as well as Kent Lee and Demi Frangela of East View Publication who obtained the Hammer papers for me from the KGB archives and Harvey Klehr, who generously supplied me documents from his Comintern archives.

I also wish to thank Steve Weinberg, Joseph Finder, and Robert C. Williams for their assiduous research on the Hammer family.

The book benefited greatly from Joseph Iseman legal assistance, Clifford May's editing of the *New York Times Magazine* article, Tina Bennett and Mort Janklow's agenting the book and the movie rights, Tina Brown's shrewd excerpting of parts of the book in *The New Yorker* and, most of all, Sharon DeLano's superb editing of the book.

Printed in Great Britain
by Amazon